SEA GARDEN

BY

H. D.

ISBN-13:
978-1534948174

ISBN-10:
1534948171

CONTENTS

Sea Rose
The Helmsman
The Shrine
Mid-day
Pursuit
The Contest
Sea Lily
The Wind Sleepers
The Gift
Evening
Sheltered Garden
Sea Poppies
Loss
Huntress
Garden
Sea Violet
The Cliff Temple
Orchard
Sea Gods
Acon
Night
Prisoners
Storm
Sea Iris
Hermes of the Ways
Pear Tree
Cities
The City is peopled

SEA GARDEN

SEA ROSE

Rose, harsh rose, marred and with stint of petals, meagre flower, thin, sparse of leaf,
more precious than a wet rose single on a stem— you are caught in the drift.
Stunted, with small leaf, you are flung on the sand, you are lifted in the crisp sand that drives in the wind.
Can the spice-rose drip such acrid fragrance hardened in a leaf?

THE HELMSMAN

O be swift— we have always known you wanted us.
We fled inland with our flocks, we pastured them in hollows, cut off from the wind and the salt track of the marsh.
We worshipped inland— we stepped past wood-flowers, we forgot your tang, we brushed wood-grass.
We wandered from pine-hills through oak and scrub-oak tangles, we broke hyssop and bramble, we caught flower and new bramble-fruit in our hair: we laughed as each branch whipped back, we tore our feet in half buried rocks and knotted roots and acorn-cups.
We forgot—we worshipped, we parted green from green, we sought further thickets, we dipped our ankles through leaf-mould and earth, and wood and wood-bank enchanted us—
and the feel of the clefts in the bark, and the slope between tree and tree— and a slender path strung field to field and wood to wood and hill to hill and the forest after it.
We forgot—for a moment tree-resin, tree-bark, sweat of a torn branch were sweet to the taste.
We were enchanted with the fields, the tufts of coarse grass in the shorter grass— we loved all this.
But now, our boat climbs—hesitates—drops— climbs—hesitates—crawls back— climbs—hesitates— O be swift— we have always known you wanted us.

THE SHRINE

("she watches over the sea")

I

Are your rocks shelter for ships— have you sent galleys from your beach, are you graded—a safe crescent— where the tide lifts them back to port— are you full and sweet, tempting the quiet to depart in their trading ships?
Nay, you are great, fierce, evil— you are the land-blight— you have tempted men but they perished on your cliffs.
Your lights are but dank shoals, slate and pebble and wet shells and seaweed fastened to the rocks.
It was evil—evil when they found you, when the quiet men looked at you— they sought a headland shaded with ledge of cliff from the wind-blast.
But you—you are unsheltered, cut with the weight of wind— you shudder when it strikes, then lift, swelled with the blast— you sink as the tide sinks, you shrill under hail, and sound thunder when thunder sounds. You are useless— when the tides swirl your boulders cut and wreck the staggering ships.

II

You are useless, O grave, O beautiful, the landsmen tell it—I have heard— you are useless.
And the wind sounds with this and the sea where rollers shot with blue cut under deeper blue.
O but stay tender, enchanted where wave-lengths cut you apart from all the rest— for we have found you, we watch the splendour of you, we thread throat on throat of freesia for your shelf.
You are not forgot, O plunder of lilies, honey is not more sweet than the salt stretch of your beach.

III

Stay—stay— but terror has caught us now, we passed the men in ships, we dared deeper than the fisher-folk and you strike us with terror O bright shaft.
Flame passes under us and sparks that unknot the flesh, sorrow, splitting bone from bone, splendour athwart our eyes and rifts in the splendour, sparks and scattered light.
Many warned of this, men said: there are wrecks on the fore-beach, wind will beat your ship, there is no shelter in that headland, it is useless waste, that edge, that front of rock— sea-gulls clang beyond the breakers, none venture to that spot.

IV

But hail— as the tide slackens, as the wind beats out, we hail this shore— we sing to you, spirit between the headlands and the further rocks.
Though oak-beams split, though boats and sea-men flounder, and the strait grind sand with sand and cut boulders to sand and drift—
your eyes have pardoned our faults, your hands have touched us— you have leaned forward a little and the waves can never thrust us back from the splendour of your ragged coast.

MID-DAY

The light beats upon me. I am startled— a split leaf crackles on the paved floor— I am anguished—defeated.
A slight wind shakes the seed-pods— my thoughts are spent as the black seeds. My thoughts tear me, I dread their fever. I am scattered in its whirl. I am scattered like the hot shrivelled seeds.
The shrivelled seeds are spilt on the path— the grass bends with dust, the grape slips under its crackled leaf: yet far beyond the spent seed-pods, and the blackened stalks of mint, the poplar is bright on the hill, the poplar spreads out, deep-rooted among trees.
O poplar, you are great among the hill-stones, while I perish on the path among the crevices of the rocks.

PURSUIT

What do I care that the stream is trampled, the sand on the stream-bank still holds the print of your foot: the heel is cut deep. I see another mark on the grass ridge of the bank— it points toward the wood-path. I have lost the third in the packed earth.
But here a wild-hyacinth stalk is snapped: the purple buds—half ripe— show deep purple where your heel pressed.
A patch of flowering grass, low, trailing— you brushed this: the green stems show yellow-green where you lifted—turned the earth-side to the light: this and a dead leaf-spine, split across, show where you passed.
You were swift, swift! here the forest ledge slopes— rain has furrowed the roots. Your hand caught at this; the root snapped under your weight.
I can almost follow the note where it touched this slender tree and the next answered— and the next.
And you climbed yet further! you stopped by the dwarf-cornel— whirled on your heels, doubled on your track.
This is clear— you fell on the downward slope, you dragged a bruised thigh—you limped— you clutched this larch.
Did your head, bent back, search further— clear through the green leaf-moss of the larch branches?
Did you clutch, stammer with short breath and gasp: *wood-daemons grant life— give life—I am almost lost.*
For some wood-daemon has lightened your steps. I can find no trace of you in the larch-cones and the underbrush.

THE CONTEST

I

Your stature is modelled with straight tool-edge: you are chiselled like rocks that are eaten into by the sea.
With the turn and grasp of your wrist and the chords' stretch, there is a glint like worn brass.
The ridge of your breast is taut, and under each the shadow is sharp, and between the clenched muscles of your slender hips.
From the circle of your cropped hair there is light, and about your male torse and the foot-arch and the straight ankle.

II

You stand rigid and mighty— granite and the ore in rocks; a great band clasps your forehead and its heavy twists of gold.
You are white—a limb of cypress bent under a weight of snow.
You are splendid, your arms are fire; you have entered the hill-straits— a sea treads upon the hill-slopes.

III

Myrtle is about your head, you have bent and caught the spray: each leaf is sharp against the lift and furrow of your bound hair.
The narcissus has copied the arch of your slight breast: your feet are citron-flowers, your knees, cut from white-ash, your thighs are rock-cistus.
Your chin lifts straight from the hollow of your curved throat. Your shoulders are level— they have melted rare silver for their breadth.

SEA LILY

Reed, slashed and torn but doubly rich— such great heads as yours drift upon temple-steps, but you are shattered in the wind.
Myrtle-bark is flecked from you, scales are dashed from your stem, sand cuts your petal, furrows it with hard edge, like flint on a bright stone.
Yet though the whole wind slash at your bark, you are lifted up, aye— though it hiss to cover you with froth.

THE WIND SLEEPERS

Whiter than the crust left by the tide, we are stung by the hurled sand and the broken shells.
We no longer sleep in the wind— we awoke and fled through the city gate.
Tear— tear us an altar, tug at the cliff-boulders, pile them with the rough stones— we no longer sleep in the wind, propitiate us.
Chant in a wail that never halts, pace a circle and pay tribute with a song. When the roar of a dropped wave breaks into it, pour meted words of sea-hawks and gulls and sea-birds that cry discords.

THE GIFT

Instead of pearls—a wrought clasp— a bracelet—will you accept this?
You know the script— you will start, wonder: what is left, what phrase after last night? This:
The world is yet unspoiled for you, you wait, expectant— you are like the children who haunt your own steps for chance bits—a comb that may have slipped, a gold tassel, unravelled, plucked from your scarf, twirled by your slight fingers into the street— a flower dropped.
Do not think me unaware, I who have snatched at you as the street-child clutched at the seed-pearls you spilt that hot day when your necklace snapped.

Do not dream that I speak as one defrauded of delight, sick, shaken by each heart-beat or paralyzed, stretched at length, who gasps: these ripe pears are bitter to the taste, this spiced wine, poison, corrupt. I cannot walk— who would walk? Life is a scavenger's pit—I escape— I only, rejecting it, lying here on this couch.
Your garden sloped to the beach, myrtle overran the paths, honey and amber flecked each leaf, the citron-lily head— one among many— weighed there, over-sweet.
The myrrh-hyacinth spread across low slopes, violets streaked black ridges through the grass.
The house, too, was like this, over painted, over lovely— the world is like this.
Sleepless nights, I remember the initiates, their gesture, their calm glance. I have heard how in rapt thought, in vision, they speak with another race, more beautiful, more intense than this. I could laugh— more beautiful, more intense?
Perhaps that other life is contrast always to this. I reason: I have lived as they in their inmost rites— they endure the tense nerves through the moment of ritual. I endure from moment to moment— days pass all alike, tortured, intense.
This I forgot last night: you must not be blamed, it is not your fault; as a child, a flower—any flower tore my breast— meadow-chicory, a common grass-tip, a leaf shadow, a flower tint unexpected on a winter-branch.
I reason: another life holds what this lacks, a sea, unmoving, quiet— not forcing our strength to rise to it, beat on beat— stretch of sand, no garden beyond, strangling with its myrrh-lilies— a hill, not set with black violets but stones, stones, bare rocks, dwarf-trees, twisted, no beauty to distract— to crowd madness upon madness.
Only a still place and perhaps some outer horror some hideousness to stamp beauty, a mark—no changing it now— on our hearts.
I send no string of pearls, no bracelet—accept this.

EVENING

The light passes from ridge to ridge, from flower to flower— the hypaticas, wide-spread under the light grow faint— the petals reach inward, the blue tips bend toward the bluer heart and the flowers are lost.
The cornel-buds are still white, but shadows dart from the cornel-roots— black creeps from root to root, each leaf cuts another leaf on the grass, shadow seeks shadow, then both leaf and leaf-shadow are lost.

SHELTERED GARDEN

I have had enough. I gasp for breath.
Every way ends, every road, every foot-path leads at last to the hill-crest— then you retrace your steps, or find the same slope on the other side, precipitate.
I have had enough— border-pinks, clove-pinks, wax-lilies, herbs, sweet-cress.
O for some sharp swish of a branch— there is no scent of resin in this place, no taste of bark, of coarse weeds, aromatic, astringent— only border on border of scented pinks.
Have you seen fruit under cover that wanted light— pears wadded in cloth, protected from the frost, melons, almost ripe, smothered in straw?
Why not let the pears cling to the empty branch? All your coaxing will only make a bitter fruit— let them cling, ripen of themselves, test their own worth, nipped, shrivelled by the frost, to fall at last but fair with a russet coat.
Or the melon— let it bleach yellow in the winter light, even tart to the taste— it is better to taste of frost— the exquisite frost— than of wadding and of dead grass.
For this beauty, beauty without strength, chokes out life. I want wind to break, scatter these pink-stalks, snap off their spiced heads, fling them about with dead leaves— spread the paths with twigs, limbs broken off, trail great pine branches, hurled from some far wood right across the melon-patch, break pear and quince— leave half-trees, torn, twisted but showing the fight was valiant.
O to blot out this garden to forget, to find a new beauty in some terrible wind-tortured place.

SEA POPPIES

Amber husk fluted with gold, fruit on the sand marked with a rich grain, treasure spilled near the shrub-pines to bleach on the boulders:
your stalk has caught root among wet pebbles and drift flung by the sea and grated shells and split conch-shells.
Beautiful, wide-spread, fire upon leaf, what meadow yields so fragrant a leaf as your bright leaf?

LOSS

The sea called— you faced the estuary, you were drowned as the tide passed.— I am glad of this— at least you have escaped.
The heavy sea-mist stifles me. I choke with each breath— a curious peril, this— the gods have invented curious torture for us.
One of us, pierced in the flank, dragged himself across the marsh, he tore at the bay-roots, lost hold on the crumbling bank—
Another crawled—too late— for shelter under the cliffs.
I am glad the tide swept you out, O beloved, you of all this ghastly host alone untouched, your white flesh covered with salt as with myrrh and burnt iris.
We were hemmed in this place, so few of us, so few of us to fight their sure lances, the straight thrust—effortless with slight life of muscle and shoulder.
So straight—only we were left, the four of us—somehow shut off.
And the marsh dragged one back, and another perished under the cliff, and the tide swept you out.
Your feet cut steel on the paths, I followed for the strength of life and grasp. I have seen beautiful feet but never beauty welded with strength. I marvelled at your height.
You stood almost level with the lance-bearers and so slight.

And I wondered as you clasped your shoulder-strap at the strength of your wrist and the turn of your young fingers, and the lift of your shorn locks, and the bronze of your sun-burnt neck.
All of this, and the curious knee-cap, fitted above the wrought greaves, and the sharp muscles of your back which the tunic could not cover— the outline no garment could deface.
I wonder if you knew how I watched, how I crowded before the spearsmen— but the gods wanted you, the gods wanted you back.

HUNTRESS

Come, blunt your spear with us, our pace is hot and our bare heels in the heel-prints— we stand tense—do you see— are you already beaten by the chase?
We lead the pace for the wind on the hills, the low hill is spattered with loose earth— our feet cut into the crust as with spears.
We climbed the ploughed land, dragged the seed from the clefts, broke the clods with our heels, whirled with a parched cry into the woods:
Can you come, can you come, can you follow the hound trail, can you trample the hot froth?
Spring up—sway forward— follow the quickest one, aye, though you leave the trail and drop exhausted at our feet.

GARDEN

I

You are clear O rose, cut in rock, hard as the descent of hail.
I could scrape the colour from the petals like spilt dye from a rock.
If I could break you I could break a tree.
If I could stir I could break a tree— I could break you.

II

O wind, rend open the heat, cut apart the heat, rend it to tatters.
Fruit cannot drop through this thick air— fruit cannot fall into heat that presses up and blunts the points of pears and rounds the grapes.
Cut the heat— plough through it, turning it on either side of your path.

SEA VIOLET

The white violet is scented on its stalk, the sea-violet fragile as agate, lies fronting all the wind among the torn shells on the sand-bank.
The greater blue violets flutter on the hill, but who would change for these who would change for these one root of the white sort?
Violet your grasp is frail on the edge of the sand-hill, but you catch the light— frost, a star edges with its fire.

THE CLIFF TEMPLE

I

Great, bright portal, shelf of rock, rocks fitted in long ledges, rocks fitted to dark, to silver granite, to lighter rock— clean cut, white against white.
High—high—and no hill-goat tramples—no mountain-sheep has set foot on your fine grass; you lift, you are the world-edge, pillar for the sky-arch.
The world heaved— we are next to the sky: over us, sea-hawks shout, gulls sweep past— the terrible breakers are silent from this place.
Below us, on the rock-edge, where earth is caught in the fissures of the jagged cliff, a small tree stiffens in the gale, it bends—but its white flowers are fragrant at this height.
And under and under, the wind booms: it whistles, it thunders, it growls— it presses the grass beneath its great feet.

II

I said: for ever and for ever, must I follow you through the stones? I catch at you—you lurch: you are quicker than my hand-grasp.
I wondered at you. I shouted—dear—mysterious—beautiful— white myrtle-flesh.
I was splintered and torn: the hill-path mounted swifter than my feet.
Could a daemon avenge this hurt, I would cry to him—could a ghost, I would shout—O evil, follow this god, taunt him with his evil and his vice.

III

Shall I hurl myself from here, shall I leap and be nearer you? Shall I drop, beloved, beloved, ankle against ankle? Would you pity me, O white breast?
If I woke, would you pity me, would our eyes meet?
Have you heard, do you know how I climbed this rock? My breath caught, I lurched forward— stumbled in the ground-myrtle.
Have you heard, O god seated on the cliff, how far toward the ledges of your house, how far I had to walk?

IV

Over me the wind swirls. I have stood on your portal and I know— you are further than this, still further on another cliff.

ORCHARD

I saw the first pear as it fell— the honey-seeking, golden-banded, the yellow swarm was not more fleet than I, (spare us from loveliness) and I fell prostrate crying: you have flayed us with your blossoms, spare us the beauty of fruit-trees.
The honey-seeking paused not, the air thundered their song, and I alone was prostrate.
O rough-hewn god of the orchard, I bring you an offering— do you, alone unbeautiful, son of the god, spare us from loveliness:
these fallen hazel-nuts, stripped late of their green sheaths, grapes, red-purple, their berries dripping with wine, pomegranates already broken, and shrunken figs and quinces untouched, I bring you as offering.

SEA GODS

I

They say there is no hope— sand—drift—rocks—rubble of the sea— the broken hulk of a ship, hung with shreds of rope, pallid under the cracked pitch.
They say there is no hope to conjure you— no whip of the tongue to anger you— no hate of words you must rise to refute.
They say you are twisted by the sea, you are cut apart by wave-break upon wave-break, that you are misshapen by the sharp rocks, broken by the rasp and after-rasp.
That you are cut, torn, mangled, torn by the stress and beat, no stronger than the strips of sand along your ragged beach.

II

But we bring violets, great masses—single, sweet, wood-violets, stream-violets, violets from a wet marsh.
Violets in clumps from hills, tufts with earth at the roots, violets tugged from rocks, blue violets, moss, cliff, river-violets.
Yellow violets' gold, burnt with a rare tint— violets like red ash among tufts of grass.
We bring deep-purple bird-foot violets.
We bring the hyacinth-violet, sweet, bare, chill to the touch— and violets whiter than the in-rush of your own white surf.

III

For you will come, you will yet haunt men in ships, you will trail across the fringe of strait and circle the jagged rocks.
You will trail across the rocks and wash them with your salt, you will curl between sand-hills— you will thunder along the cliff— break—retreat— get fresh strength— gather and pour weight upon the beach.
You will draw back, and the ripple on the sand-shelf will be witness of your track.
 O privet-white, you will paint the lintel of wet sand with froth.
You will bring myrrh-bark and drift laurel-wood from hot coasts! when you hurl high—high— we will answer with a shout.

For you will come, you will come, you will answer our taut hearts, you will break the lie of men's thoughts, and cherish and shelter us.

ACON

I

Bear me to Dictaeus, and to the steep slopes; to the river Erymanthus.
I choose spray of dittany, cyperum, frail of flower, buds of myrrh, all-healing herbs, close pressed in calathes.
For she lies panting, drawing sharp breath, broken with harsh sobs, she, Hyella, whom no god pities.

II

Dryads haunting the groves, nereids who dwell in wet caves, for all the white leaves of olive-branch, and early roses, and ivy wreaths, woven gold berries, which she once brought to your altars, bear now ripe fruits from Arcadia, and Assyrian wine to shatter her fever.
The light of her face falls from its flower, as a hyacinth, hidden in a far valley, perishes upon burnt grass.
Pales, bring gifts, bring your Phoenician stuffs, and do you, fleet-footed nymphs, bring offerings, Illyrian iris, and a branch of shrub, and frail-headed poppies.

NIGHT

The night has cut each from each and curled the petals back from the stalk and under it in crisp rows;
under at an unfaltering pace, under till the rinds break, back till each bent leaf is parted from its stalk;
under at a grave pace, under till the leaves are bent back till they drop upon earth, back till they are all broken.
O night, you take the petals of the roses in your hand, but leave the stark core of the rose to perish on the branch.

PRISONERS

It is strange that I should want this sight of your face— we have had so much: at any moment now I may pass, stand near the gate, do not speak— only reach if you can, your face half-fronting the passage toward the light.
Fate—God sends this as a mark, a last token that we are not forgot, lost in this turmoil, about to be crushed out, burned or stamped out at best with sudden death.
The spearsman who brings this will ask for the gold clasp you wear under your coat. I gave all I had left.
Press close to the portal, my gate will soon clang and your fellow wretches will crowd to the entrance— be first at the gate.
Ah beloved, do not speak. I write this in great haste— do not speak, you may yet be released. I am glad enough to depart though I have never tasted life as in these last weeks.
It is a strange life, patterned in fire and letters on the prison pavement. If I glance up it is written on the walls, it is cut on the floor, it is patterned across the slope of the roof.
I am weak—weak— last night if the guard had left the gate unlocked I could not have ventured to escape, but one thought serves me now with strength.
As I pass down the corridor past desperate faces at each cell, your eyes and my eyes may meet.
You will be dark, unkempt, but I pray for one glimpse of your face— why do I want this? I who have seen you at the banquet each flower of your hyacinth-circlet white against your hair.

Why do I want this, when even last night you startled me from sleep? You stood against the dark rock, you grasped an elder staff.
So many nights you have distracted me from terror. Once you lifted a spear-flower. I remember how you stooped to gather it— and it flamed, the leaf and shoot and the threads, yellow, yellow— sheer till they burnt to red-purple in the cup.
As I pass your cell-door do not speak. I was first on the list— They may forget you tried to shield me as the horsemen passed.

STORM

You crash over the trees, you crack the live branch— the branch is white, the green crushed, each leaf is rent like split wood.
You burden the trees with black drops, you swirl and crash— you have broken off a weighted leaf in the wind, it is hurled out, whirls up and sinks, a green stone.

SEA IRIS

I

Weed, moss-weed, root tangled in sand, sea-iris, brittle flower, one petal like a shell is broken, and you print a shadow like a thin twig.
Fortunate one, scented and stinging, rigid myrrh-bud, camphor-flower, sweet and salt—you are wind in our nostrils.

II

Do the murex-fishers drench you as they pass? Do your roots drag up colour from the sand? Have they slipped gold under you— rivets of gold? Band of iris-flowers above the waves, you are painted blue, painted like a fresh prow stained among the salt weeds.

HERMES OF THE WAYS

The hard sand breaks, and the grains of it are clear as wine.
Far off over the leagues of it, the wind, playing on the wide shore, piles little ridges, and the great waves break over it.
But more than the many-foamed ways of the sea, I know him of the triple path-ways, Hermes, who awaits.
Dubious, facing three ways, welcoming wayfarers, he whom the sea-orchard shelters from the west, from the east weathers sea-wind; fronts the great dunes.
Wind rushes over the dunes, and the coarse, salt-crusted grass answers.
Heu, it whips round my ankles!

II

Small is this white stream, flowing below ground from the poplar-shaded hill, but the water is sweet.
Apples on the small trees are hard, too small, too late ripened by a desperate sun that struggles through sea-mist.
The boughs of the trees are twisted by many bafflings; twisted are the small-leafed boughs.
But the shadow of them is not the shadow of the mast head nor of the torn sails.
Hermes, Hermes, the great sea foamed, gnashed its teeth about me; but you have waited, were sea-grass tangles with shore-grass.

PEAR TREE

Silver dust lifted from the earth, higher than my arms reach, you have mounted, O silver, higher than my arms reach you front us with great mass;
no flower ever opened so staunch a white leaf, no flower ever parted silver from such rare silver;
O white pear, your flower-tufts thick on the branch bring summer and ripe fruits in their purple hearts.

CITIES

Can we believe—by an effort comfort our hearts: it is not waste all this, not placed here in disgust, street after street, each patterned alike, no grace to lighten a single house of the hundred crowded into one garden-space. Crowded—can we believe, not in utter disgust, in ironical play— but the maker of cities grew faint with the beauty of temple and space before temple, arch upon perfect arch, of pillars and corridors that led out to strange court-yards and porches where sun-light stamped hyacinth-shadows black on the pavement.
That the maker of cities grew faint with the splendour of palaces, paused while the incense-flowers from the incense-trees dropped on the marble-walk, thought anew, fashioned this— street after street alike.
For alas, he had crowded the city so full that men could not grasp beauty, beauty was over them, through them, about them, no crevice unpacked with the honey, rare, measureless.
So he built a new city, ah can we believe, not ironically but for new splendour constructed new people to lift through slow growth to a beauty unrivalled yet— and created new cells, hideous first, hideous now— spread larve across them, not honey but seething life.
And in these dark cells, packed street after street, souls live, hideous yet— O disfigured, defaced, with no trace of the beauty men once held so light.
Can we think a few old cells were left—we are left— grains of honey, old dust of stray pollen dull on our torn wings, we are left to recall the old streets?
Is our task the less sweet that the larve still sleep in their cells? Or crawl out to attack our frail strength: You are useless. We live. We await great

events. We are spread through this earth. We protect our strong race. You are useless. Your cell takes the place of our young future strength. Though they sleep or wake to torment and wish to displace our old cells— thin rare gold— that their larve grow fat— is our task the less sweet? Though we wander about, find no honey of flowers in this waste, is our task the less sweet— who recall the old splendour, await the new beauty of cities?

The city is peopled with spirits, not ghosts, O my love:
Though they crowded between and usurped the kiss of my mouth their breath was your gift, their beauty, your life.

CPSIA information can be obtained
at www.ICGtesting.com
Printed in the USA
LVHW10s1518060918
589351LV00014B/294/P